Bleed To Heal

TAHMEENA SARKAR

I wrote this book for the ones who lost themselves in the process of getting over someone or something that never truly belonged to them, to make them feel found, whole, and healed.

Contents

Foreword

Dear reader,

I put all my pieces
in your hand
to find their home
in your heart.
I hope you will let them.
I hope you will handle them with care.

Bleed

Love

• 3 •

I had drunk you.
Now,
I have to bleed you as well.

· 4 ·

When someone smells like home, it's called Love.
- **What is Love?**

• 5 •

There is little difference
between a house and a home.
A house is what humans make
and a home is what humans are made of.
- *What is home?*

• 6 •

Love has no magic,
Love itself is magic.
You need love even to forget
the love you lost.
- *Learn to bleed love.*

• 7 •

You are everything
I could Love,
The melody of the sea,
a cup of tea, and
a book of poetry.

Be my half poetry,
I will be your full story;
The story that
will fill you with warmth,
give you light and
build your home within.
- *A Proposal*

• 9 •

Just like Venus,

you are hotter than the universe.

- *A Compliment*

I am the rain lily
seeking rain to bloom.
- *You are the rain.*

• 11 •

They think
I am obsessed with poetry,
but nobody knows
I named you one.

I hope
you will see the flowers
blooming inside me.
I hope
you will see the fire
burning inside me.
I hope
you will see both sides.
I hope!

• 13 •

I'm obsessed with the moon, stars,
clouds, sunrises, sunsets, rainbows,
and everything that belongs to the sky or
everything far from me.

The sea and you
have so much in common:
both always seem
fresh and new.

• 15 •

I adore
every shade of blue
like the sea, sky,
and you.

Meet me here
or somewhere else,
but meet me under the burning sky
where our souls chase nothing
but light.

The full moon
and the blue sky
remind me of nothing
but you;
the pure you,
the naive you,
and most importantly,
the rare you.

I hope they remind you of me
in the same way.

Be the Mercury
to the Sun inside me.
Stay too close
to bear my sparks,
or let yourself burn.

I wish

there was a world made of poetry,

I mean, made of you.

You are my living poetry with bones and muscles.

I could burn
in order to shine for you.
I could run miles
if I have to find you.
I could stay long
at the same place
with the same old heart
as well as love,
to welcome you.
If you ever decide
to come back home,
you will always find me there
at the doorstep.
I'm all yours,
I'm all yours.

It was a winter Sunday morning.
I opened the window
to feel the morning breeze.
He held me from the back
and rolled his finger on my neck
before we were almost close
to kiss each other's lips.
Mom woke me up.
-A dream I always wanted to live in.

Meet me at the closure.
We will write the ending together.
- **Will you?**

Evening comes early
and night stays longer.
Sometimes, the temperature
gets as high as hell.
But sometimes,
it rains all day long.
How a soft, delightful woman
gave birth to a chaotic woman
in this terrific month.
- ***September.***

Without the fear of
being apart
or losing each other,
just like the moon
loves the ocean,
a sunflower does the same
for the sun
can't even be together
but made for each other.
We loved that much,
we dreamt that much.

• 25 •

Isn't it beautiful,
How a thousand people's happiness
might be caused by an imperfect moon?
- Eid

The woman

with sunflowers in her eyes

and autumn dancing in her hair;

The wrinkles on her face

are not just a sign of her age

but the art she creates

with love and light.

Her 80s feet don't allow her to walk,

but her evergreen words

could give you the wings to fly or rise.

Her father named her Flower,

but she is not just a flower;

a whole garden lies in her.

She is no one but the manifester

of the man who raised a woman

totally opposite of her.

- Grandmother

A woman in love
could do both:
write an entire book for you
or kill you with silence.

I am the ocean
Manifesting tsunamis
to bring you back
to your origin.

• 29 •

I became a poet
when all I wanted was
to be a poem
written by you.

Nobody will ever write you
into poetry the way I do.

I am so jealous of you
for having a lover
like me.

• 31 •

When darkness engulfed me
and the stars beckoned me
to make a wish,
I whispered your name
instead of wanting light.

• 32 •

I will follow you
like a firefly;
In your darkest night,
I would be your only light.

Bleed

Pain

• 35 •

Bleed pain and
let your aches flow out
from your veins.

Pour out your pain.
That's how poetry happens.

I was the ocean of love
and he was bad
at swimming.

I saw him
with another woman;
holding her hand
more wisely and more lovingly.
Trust me,
my eyes had never witnessed
a disaster or an act of terrorism
like this before.

It's hard to decide which is worse:
Seeing you sad or
seeing you happy with someone else.

On anyone else's arm,
I will still feel
like I am cheating on you,
even though it was you
who did it years ago.

• 41 •

I let you go
to let me grow.

I just wish to feel
the same love I gave.
- *Is it a crime?*

I don't know if I am
too empty or
holding too much
to let love in.

• 44 •

I will try to
forget you tomorrow.

Let me love you today,
a little more than yesterday.

You were good.
But maybe the universe is
planning to give me the best.

- Genuine optimism

Probably, it was in the last days of July,
when the blazing sun abruptly turned into gray
and descended to earth to greet him
in a most beautiful way.
I saw a guy with a checked shirt
and blue jeans step out of the car
and open the door for me with a smile.
- I never thought heartache would begin this way.

• 47 •

You taught me both
how to love and
how to leave.

• 48 •

I'm still learning how to tell you,
I miss you while telling you I don't.

• 49 •

A night of June
when the sky was surviving
without the moon;
It was raining outside,
ruining inside as well.
The wet leaves and
the gentle breeze
after the rain
were trying to turn off my pain.
A night of June
when the sky was surviving
without the moon.

I was so wrong
to think you were my destiny
when you were destined
not to be.

He caused me
mountains of pain
and yet expected me
to carry them all
with silence.
- But I choose to rise.

I made you my sunshine
without knowing
I was the dewdrop
that could vanish in it.

I'm homesick for the home
I'm barely welcome in.

Some are chasing canopies,
Some are waiting for sunshine
and here I am craving
for that fallen star.

• 55 •

It took me years
to turn off my tears.
But your eyes took just a second
to take me back
to day one.

• 56 •

You were the full moon to me,
But I was the Venus
you were unworthy of.

• 57 •

You took half of me away,
And the rest of me
Isn't me anymore.

I don't know
what you deserve;
But one day you will chase
my kind of love.
That blue,
that pure.

• 59 •

He caused the earthquake
and then blamed me
for the damages.

There are so many stories
I could share,
so much love to give,
so much time to spend.
But you left too soon.
You left too soon.

I was the coast
And you were the wave.
We briefly met
and then parted ways.

• 62 •

My heart has never wept
more than the day
you decided
not to stay anymore.

He started to hate me
because I told his homies
how he broke my home.
After all, we humans hate to be exposed.

• 64 •

Reality sucks,
but
hope fools twice.

• 65 •

Inked this for you,
but I'm scared
my poetry would remind
you of someone else.

How foolish of me
to write page after page
for someone
who never wanted
to read me.

• 67 •

I waited longer
than you had stayed.

It seems
we were both wrong in ways:
me for loving you too much and
you for loving me too less.

• 69 •

Whenever you caused me pain,
I bled poetry
over and over again.

I wish

you had stayed a little longer;
I would have loved you a little deeper.
I wish you had stayed a little longer;
I would have hugged you a little harder.
I wish you had stayed a little longer,
I would have convinced you
to stay a bit longer than forever.
I wish you had stayed.
I wish!

I wonder which pains more:
your leaving,
or the way you made me feel
replaced.

I see the rainstorm
in her eyes,
where once I saw
the rainbow.

Tahmeena Sarkar

I love poetry
from the very beginning,
But it hits different
after you left.

After years of separation,
whenever I see you,
I feel the same way
I used to:
You still make my heart beat faster,
cause an earthquake in my bones,
make my veins a little jumpy,
and make me feel giddy,
like I am excited and nervous
at the same time.
Tell me, what is it
if not love?

Once you were my poetry,
now you are in my poetry.
I conceal you from the world
with every word I say.

How could I love you
when I'm already unloved
by someone else?
How could I let you in
when my roots are still shaking?
Let me heal first
to heal you.
Let me be fixed first
to fix you.
Let me love myself first
to love you.
- Denying a proposal

I forgive you,
but I am not truly able to forget you.
What if you return someday
and I'm not around
to greet you at all?

The day you departed
caused me less pain
than the day
I learned
you wouldn't return.

You are like a storm:
Stayed a while
but destroyed me
forever.

The chaos I have been carrying
inside my heart
needs the taste of you
to survive.

About the day we last met,
all I can recall is that
I felt unfamiliar looking into those eyes
where I once felt at home.

The saddest thing is,
I would have to die
with this anguish.

I wish I could say all the ways
I have ever suffered.
And I wish
you could understand
without any words.

It's been years, but feels like yesterday.
The wound is real
and new
every time I think of you.

• 85 •

I paid a huge amount
to find myself
by losing you.

The place where
we met for the last time
still reminds me of you.
Those eyes
full of hate,
Words full of wounds,
and the
face full of suspense.

I was living my life around you,
and now I'm just getting by.

I hope you are aware of the distinction.

Even after enduring
all the suffering you caused,
my heart is still not ready to release you.
- How could something be that strong?

Little did I know
you are the Saturn
before thinking
I'm the only moon you have.
-Mistake

Long before March,
he decided to embrace spring
without extinguishing the winter fire
he once set her heart on.
-The beginning of the ending.

And
I fought
with you
for you.

He wanted space
when I made him
my constellation.

• 93 •

You can't force someone
to unlove you
just because you regret
not loving them back.

A piece of my heart
will always beat for you.
No matter how much time has passed
or how far I have come.

• 95 •

My room is full of you;
I wish it could have a single place
for someone new.

Have you ever felt
as if you have done anything wrong
to someone who gave you
the greatest amount of belief
when you glanced in the mirror?
- *I guess never.*

I hold the pen to
unfold my pain.

It was the middle of October
I felt the autumn very hard
by letting you go.

• 99 •

I loved you
and let you love whoever
you want to.

In the name of goodbye,
he took my home away.
Where should I go now?

You left me
over the same reason
once you loved me for.
- Having too much love to give.

All of a sudden, you began to ignore me, argue with me about every little thing, and blame me for everything. I started to overthink, believing that perhaps it was my fault and that you needed more time to work things out. All the while, I was trying to fit into your world to fix everything. But, in the end, you broke my trust and threw me out of your life like dust. Like I never deserved to love, like I was never enough to love.

- You murdered a soul, accept it.

I know,

one day I will be able to release you

from every corner of my heart and my mind.

I know,

one day these feelings will be foreign

and the experiences will expire.

I know,

one day your presence will not make me feel excited

and your absence will not make me bleed anymore.

I know.

I know.

We are now two distinct worlds,
under the same moon.

You turned me
into your kingdom to rule over
and abandoned me
to become a battlefield.

You told me that you loved me and took less than a week to love someone else. Tell me, what kind of love was it? If you can't love someone in their absence, then you literally don't know what love actually means.

Tell me, how many times
would I have to bleed
to not bleed again?

The day I will
heal is when your
name doesn't
make me bleed.

Bleed

To

Heal

• 111 •

Never bleed to death;
Bleed pain, bleed poetry,
bleed love or
whatever, you bleed,
bleed to heal,
bleed to survive.

I was just trying to hold
someone else's home
- *Realization*

You are not healing
because you are still
watering the pain.
Let the pain
run away
just like the person did.

It's okay; rain lilies are not
less beautiful than sunflowers.
And the best part is,
you can be both.

When you can be the entire sky, why do you need wings to fly? Within you lies an entire sky filled with stars of hope, clouds of joy, a sun of strength, and a full moon of magic. You are enough and everything at once.

I hope this piece
will keep my love
alive after I am gone.

• 117 •

Give up begging;
You are not the one.
Start raging.
You belong to the ocean.

Be the wave
that touches the clouds
before reaching the shore.

Isn't it admirable
to part ways with someone
who never was yours in the first place?

My words
will draw
the bow
you have been seeking for.

Indeed,
no one will ever love them
the way you did.
But perhaps someone is
already giving them the kind of love
they desire.
- *Think in a new way.*

Stop chasing that fallen star;
galaxies have so much more
to offer.

Don't be harsh;
Be more kind,
and more loving;
Make them regret
what they lost.

How beautiful
it is to be dreaming
of flying
while the entire sky is
already draped over her shoulders.

She is merely a planet;
Hotter and brighter,
yet less than a star.
Too near to worship the sun
but distances herself from the moon,
as she knows how to shine without one.
Indeed, she is just a planet, nothing more.
However, something more than the galaxies long for.

-Venus.

It's necessary
to feel pain
because you will
never know the worth
of sunshine
without going
through a storm.

If you can't
endure the night,
you don't deserve
the moon either.

Like a bottle of whisky or
a plate of dessert,
you are born to be desired.
There is a pretty reason
for your existence.
Never lose hope;
The magic is near,
the universe is here
on your way.

• 129 •

Being the sun
and having
your own light
to shine is rare
and divine.

To the one
who created a void in my heart,
who left me in despair,
who broke me beyond repair:
I am TAHMEENA
which means 'Strong and Powerful'.
My name is enough to
remind you;
I'm the hurricane raging inside,
I'm the ocean brimming with light.
I'm the healer,
I'm the teacher,
I'm the survivor.

• 131 •

It's okay
to feel,
to fall,
to be broken,
but it is mandatory
to rise
all over again.

You aren't half.
You are just a little
far from whole.
You are the moon,
incomplete yet
terrifically beautiful.

After surviving
the forest fires,
I described
everything poetically.
-Is it easy to be a writer?

The whole world
might think it's common
to have pain, but
only you know
the depths of it.
So, take your time
and grieve
as much as you can
to relieve your heart
and embrace
your soul.

Tahmeena Sarkar

Don't keep anything
inside you
that could harm you later.
If you don't have
anyone to tell,
share it with paper.
Lift your pen
and bleed
whatever leads you
to the verse
of the last breath.
Don't let the ashes
build a home in you.
Break them and help them
to leave you,
and let yourself
live,
rise,
soar.

You should be proud of yourself for carrying such a kind soul in this cruel world. Souls like you deserve the golden light of a paddy field, or the pure, blue sky after rain. You deserve a room full of old books, or a bouquet full of lilies. You deserve a handwritten love note with your favorite dish, or a dress gifted from your wishlist. Never settle for less; you are the external manifestation of love, light, and hope. You deserve everything and anything more than this.

Never hate yourself for loving them too much. Who gave you only pain in return. You should be proud of yourself because you have oceans of love within you to give. You are so blessed with love. The universe has made you to spread love and kindness, that is what the world needs to survive. Even those who gave you the pain are also in pain, they don't have love to give, they don't know how to love; they are in darkness. They need you; teach them how to love, fill them with love. Baby, you are like a guardian angel, go change the world with nothing but love and love.

He named me Hurricane
and raised me like a hero.
When there is a strong man
standing behind me,
how could I not be the strongest?
-Father.

I don't want you.
I want the man I lost in you.
Tell him to come back
to his home.
I'm waiting with a cup of tea,
and I will wait until eternity.

Everyone appreciates the beauty of a butterfly, but no one notices the effort of a firefly. They light themselves just to make you feel warm in your darkest times, help you to find the right path, encourage you to never give up, and guide you to survive. Remember, beauty is less beautiful than effort.

I know you are going through a tough time when there is no one with you to give you the strength to fight or survive, but I hope you will stay there for yourself.I hope every time you will find the way back to yourself, you will choose happiness over everything and take the positive sides of all. I can feel you; I can feel the pain so deeply that you are dealing with. I am sorry if I am not with you but I know you will rise from all the ashes like a phoenix. I know you can still hold onto hope and go on like a victor. you are the bravest soul someone could ever be proud of. You can survive a storm, cyclone, then a tsunami and yet your roots will remain strong. Never underestimate your healing power. Know your worth and choose your path.

Maybe today, you are thinking you will never heal, never get the happiness you deserve, and never be able to love. But trust me, there are so many good days yet to come when you will feel alive, when you will get whatever you need, and when you will be loved the way you want. All you have to do is be patient; better days are finding their way back to you, okay?

Dear stranger,
I hope you will never get scared to heal.
I hope you will never get scared to bleed.
It's hard yet essential in order to
repair,
rebuild,
and be reborn.

Every piece of you
will bring peace to you,
and the rest of the world
will love to create
chaos in you,
so be you
and let the world
do the rest.

The pain will never leave
unless
you accept it,
feel it,
live it,
learn from it.

Plant poetry in
your sore
and wait for the
magic to cure.

I never thought
you would mean
this much to me
that after all these years,
I am still here
to bear you
all over again.

And I am here
as the gray clouds
in your sky,
filled with nothing
but rain,
to wash away
all your
pain.

• 149 •

You called me dark,
but at least I am
something that stark,
that whole,
that pure.

I will love you
till I can last
without wanting you back.

Fire or firefly,
she belongs to both.
Flame or light,
she could be both.
She is you,
she is me.

If they distract
your self-love,
cut them off,
and let yourself bleed
to bloom.

I was good enough at loving,
and you were at pretending.

• 154 •

Pain is a kind of blessing for a writer. It leads them to powerful poems that could bring hope to millions. Dear reader, I would love to live in pain to bring you hope. Trust me.

• 155 •

The day
when you felt sorry
for whatever you had done to me,
I won.

I owe you for helping me find myself, for making me stronger than ever, and for manifesting the woman I am today. I'm grateful that you left. Thank you.

www.ingramcontent.com/pod-product-compliance
Lightning Source LLC
Chambersburg PA
CBHW031136130726
47988CB00006B/2401